All About Animals

Orangutans

By Susan Kueffner

Reader's Digest Young Families

Contents

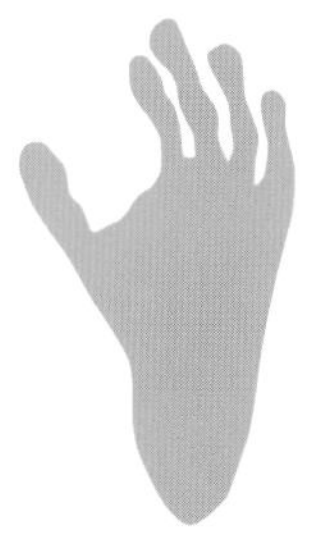

Chapter 1
A Baby Is Born

Hang On!

An orangutan child learns to hang on tightly. It has to grab for places that will give its mother's arms and legs plenty of room to move through the treetops.

The steady buzz of insects vibrates throughout the rainforest. It is interrupted only by the songs and calls of tropical birds. But suddenly a strange sound fills the air. It begins as a long, low rumble that echoes across the steamy, shadowy forest. What can it be? The sound comes once more. It builds and builds until . . . *ROAAARR!* Then it trails off into a sigh. The sound is the "long call" of a male orangutan.

A 15-year-old female orangutan moves through the vines and tree limbs, attracted by the strange sound. The male calls again, and she finds him. They mate high in the treetops, and the couple spends a few days traveling together. Then the male goes away, and the new mother-to-be continues through the forest on her own.

Eight months later it's a birthday! The tiny newborn orangutan weighs about two pounds. And although orangutans like to be alone, mother and child will be close companions for the next seven or eight years.

At first, Mama Orangutan cradles her newborn in her arms, patting his head and comforting him with soft sucking sounds. She tenderly feeds him her milk and a special orangutan baby food: leaves she has chewed into a soft mush. At night they cuddle together in a treetop nest that Mama has made of bent branches and padded with leaves. They may stay in the nest for several days, until Baby Orangutan has developed the tight grip needed to cling to Mama's fur.

In the next weeks and months, Baby Orangutan will ride piggyback on his mother or cling to her side as she swings through the trees. Around his first birthday, Mama will add fruit to his diet. He'll try to make his way over the branches by himself. But Mama Orangutan will allow this only under her watchful eye. From heights of 20 to 80 feet above the forest's floor, a fall from a vine or tree branch could cause a serious injury, or even death. If the trees are too far apart, Mama Orangutan will still carry Baby across the span. Sometimes she will form a living bridge between the trees, allowing him to scamper across on her back.

Wild Words

A **rainforest** *is a warm, wet forest, teeming with trees, flowers, insects, and wildlife. Dense leaves and vines high in the trees form a ceiling over the forest. This ceiling is called a* **canopy**.

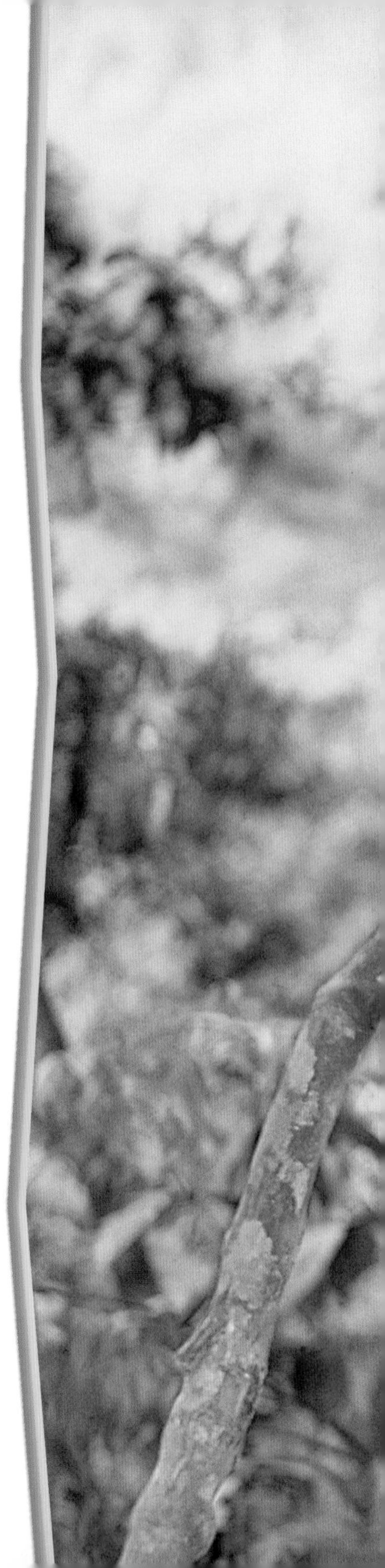

Room Service!
Most orangutans build a new sleeping nest every night as they make their way through the forest.

Occasionally, mother and child will meet another mother and child at a fruit-filled tree, and the two babies will play together. They'll pat and poke each other, chase each other up and down the trees and vines, tumble and somersault in an acrobatic dance. But the mothers will just watch, almost ignoring each other.

By the time he is four years old, Baby Orangutan begins to understand that he is growing up. Already, he can get a lot of his food on his own. He practices building his own nest, but it is always near Mama's. He won't stray far away, even if Mama should have another baby in the next year or so. He needs her lessons and her protection. Dangers, such as hungry pythons, lurk in the forest. Despite the careful and loving attention of their mothers, the survival rate of orangutan babies born in the wild is very low.

Leaving the Nest

At age seven or eight, a young orangutan is ready to live on its own. A young female may stay in or near her mother's territory or travel with other young females for a short while. When orangutans are between ten and fifteen years old, they're ready to mate. A female orangutan usually raises two to four children during her lifetime.

Chapter 2
An Orangutan's Body

Some male orangutans can spread their arms more than 7 feet wide. That's longer than the height of most professional basketball players.

Funny Faces

Imagine a fifth-grader who weighs as much as his father, whose hands reach to his feet, and who can hang from his arms for hours. That gives you a pretty good idea of the size and strength of the average male orangutan. Orangutans are large, shy apes that are the cousins of gorillas, chimpanzees, bonobos—and humans. Orangutans have 97 percent of the same DNA sequence as humans. This makes them one of man's closest relatives.

These giant apes are covered with a long, shaggy, sometimes sparse, rust-colored fur; the skin color underneath ranges from beige to brown to almost dark blue. A male weighs between 150 and 200 pounds and stands about 3 to 5 feet tall, with a thick neck, barrel chest, long arms, short bowed legs, and no tail. A female weighs about half as much and is rarely taller than 3 feet.

Funny Faces

Orangutan faces are remarkably humanlike, with endearing, sometimes frightening, and often amusing expressions.

Close-up

Male orangutans have throat sacs and cheek pads, and they develop huge rolls of fat in their cheeks. The fatter the cheeks, the more dominant the orangutan—and the more attractive he is to female orangutans.

Only Two of a Kind

The last wild orangutans on Earth live on two islands in Southeast Asia: Borneo in Indonesia and Sumatra in Malaysia. Males in Borneo generally have square-shaped faces, brownish-red fur, fatter rolls in their cheeks, and large throat sacs. Males in Sumatra have diamond-shaped faces, ginger-colored fur, and small cheek pads and throat sacs.

Hands and Feet On!

Like humans, orangutans have ten fingers and ten toes — but with an important difference. In addition to having a thumb on each hand, an orangutan has a big toe that acts like a thumb on each foot. These "foot thumbs" allow an orangutan to use its feet as if they were hands, so it can grab and hold on to things with its hands, its feet, or both.

In addition, an orangutan's legs have full circular motion, just like its arms. It can reach and stretch its legs (and arms) in an incredible number of directions and angles.

You can tell by his cheeks that this ornagutan is from Borneo.

The male orangutan's large cheek pads and throat sac makes his "long call" louder and stronger.

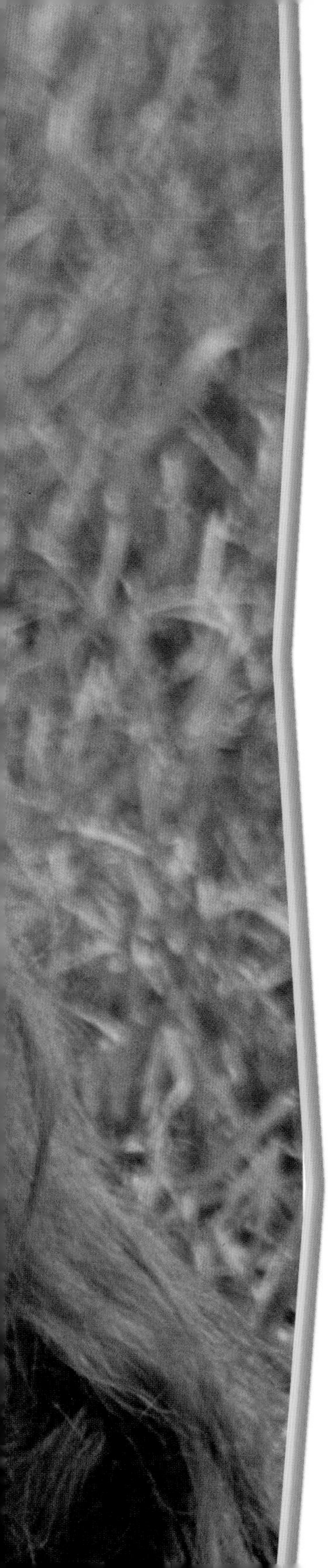

Calls of the Wild

Orangutans make about 13 vocal sounds, fewer than other primates. Scientists believe this is because orangutans usually live alone and seldom need to communicate with other orangutans. When they do have something to say, they can make noises that range from sighs to grumbling groans to ear-piercing roars. Males are famous for their "long call": a series of low roars that build to loud bellowing and then trail off again. Researchers debate whether this call is meant to attract females, warn off predators, announce the male's location, or all three. The call is so loud that humans have reported hearing it more than half a mile away.

Orangutans also communicate by their actions. They stretch and jump, arch their backs, beat their chests, smack their lips, wave their heads, and shake their arms. And watch out—they even throw things! They might bare their teeth, which can look deceptively like a smile. But don't be fooled. It's actually a sign of aggression, a rare signal from this usually gentle ape.

Chapter 3
“People of the Forest”

It takes years for a young orangutan to learn which vines and tree limbs are strong enough and flexible enough to use to travel through the forest.

What's in a Name?

In the Malay language, *orang* means "person" and *utan* means "forest." So the word *orangutan* means "people of the forest."

Going It Alone

Orangutans are loners, and they like it that way! Once grown, orangutans choose to wander through the treetops by themselves all day long. This preference for a solitary life may be because orangutans have huge appetites. A group of them traveling together would create too much competition for a limited amount of food, quickly stripping a tree of every last leaf and fruit.

Slow-motion Acrobats

Orangutans move like high-wire acrobats far up in the trees. However, because of their great weight, they cannot simply jump like a squirrel from tree to tree. Instead, they move very slowly and thoughtfully, using their weight to bend one tree limb—or even an entire tree—toward another. They reach, grab a new branch with their hands or feet, swing over, and continue on their way. Each time they move, they have to decide which limb or vine will support their weight. They might even push over a dead tree and ride it down as it falls, grabbing hold of some vines just before it crashes to the ground.

Orangutans rarely spend time on the ground. They will leave their treetop perches if the space between two trees is too wide to swing across. On the ground, orangutans "fist-walk" slowly and awkwardly, standing semi-upright and supporting their weight on their hands or fists as well as on their feet.

A Fruitful Life

Fruit is the orangutan's favorite meal. In fact, if the supply is plentiful, orangutans will happily stick to a fruit-only diet. They gobble up mangos, jackfruit, rambutan, and figs. Their favorite is the fruit of the durian tree. This large prickly fruit is about the size of a small watermelon. But under its thorny skin and very unpleasant odor lies a sweet custard that tastes a little like cheese and a little like garlic. Orangutans tear the fruit open with their strong teeth, eating the flesh and the seeds and discarding the skin. Yum!

An orangutan's diet is highly varied. In fact, it consists of more than 400 different kinds of food—and most of an orangutan's day is devoted to hunting it down.

When thirsty, orangutans find water in holes in trees. They simply reach in and scoop up a handful to drink.

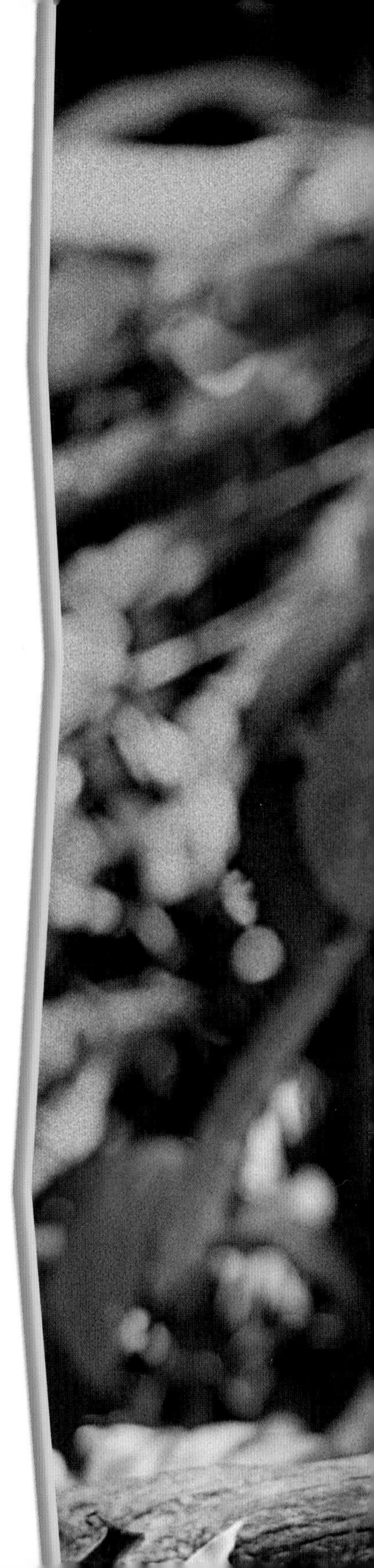

Not Too Choosy

When fruit is scarce, orangutans will eat other things, including leaves, bark, insects, flowers, and birds' eggs.

As an orangutan bites into a fruit, seeds spill to the ground. They settle into the soil and, in time, will sprout. In this way, orangutans help promote the new growth of tropical fruit trees.

It takes an orangutan less than 5 minutes to build his "nest in the sky."

Time for Bed

When darkness falls in the rainforest, the orangutan is ready for bed. However, he is rarely in the same place he was the night before, so he must build a brand-new nest, or resting place, each night.

The nest looks like a fancy, oversized bird's nest. The orangutan bends branches down and weaves them together into a somewhat level platform. He uses sticks to hold it all together and pads it with comfy leaves. He may add a pile of twigs and leaves as a pillow and perhaps a roof of branches to protect himself from heavy rain. He makes smacking and clicking sounds as he builds and offers self-satisfied "raspberries" (spluttering through his lips) when he's finished. The nest makes a cozy bed for one, built anywhere from 20 to 80 feet above the ground. It is rarely shared, except between a mother and her child or between mating adults.

Nests help scientists monitor how many orangutans are alive. Since these giant apes blend into the shadows overhead, they're difficult to count by observation. Their nests are not. Researchers count nests in limited areas and enter that information into a specialized computer program to estimate the size of the orangutan population.

Chapter 4
Orangutan Intelligence

Orangutans are capable of finding "tools" that are the perfect size to poke into tiny insect hiding places.

Smart Thinking!

Scientists have long observed orangutans using sticks and leaves as tools, proof of their high level of intelligence. For example, an orangutan will poke a twig into a hole in a tree trunk, jiggle it around, and pull it out covered with insects—a creepy-crawly popsicle! Orangutans also use sticks as backscratchers or as "fishing poles" to knock fruit they can't reach off a tree. They're good problem-solvers too. Orangutans can't swim very well, so they use a long stick or pole to check the depth of the water before crossing a river.

Young orangutans watch their mothers and learn to use leaves as napkins to wipe their chins or as washcloths to rub dirt off their bodies. They use curled leaves as cups to scoop up water. They also learn that leaves can be used as gloves for handling prickly fruits.

Don't Rain on Me!
Orangutans don't like to get wet, so they use leafy branches as tropical umbrellas. Sometimes they even build leafy roofs over their sleeping nests to help keep them dry at night.

The Aha! Factor

Scientists have observed that orangutans seem to have a mysterious internal thought-process that differs from that of the other great apes. For example, if chimpanzees are given an oddly shaped peg and several holes to put it in, they will approach the problem by trial-and-error. They will insert the peg into each hole until they come to the one it fits. In contrast, an orangutan will look at the problem, stare off into space for a while, and then stick the peg into the correct hole! How does the orangutan do it? No one knows for sure.

Rainforest Defenses

Orangutans are generally peaceful animals, but when threatened, they won't hesitate to defend themselves. And what do they use as weapons? They use whatever is available—and in the rainforest, that means tree limbs. In the hands of an orangutan, a big limb dropped from high in the treetops can be used as a missile to scare off humans.

A male orangutan might fling a branch at another male who seems to be moving in on his territory or his mate. A mother orangutan uses sticks and branches to protect her baby from a snake or a bird. Orangutans even use dead trees as weapons, knocking them over onto intruders with a crash!

An orangutan can hold on to vines and limbs firmly with its feet as well as its hands.

One of the ways orangutans learn to do things is by imitation. No wonder that the verb "ape" is just another way of saying "imitate."

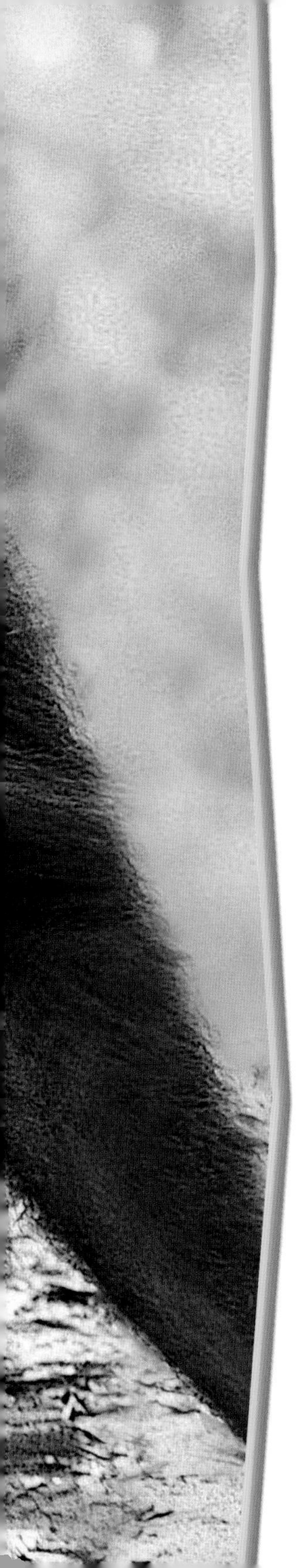

The Great Imitators

How do orangutans learn? They copy what they see others doing. After watching villagers handle their canoes, orangutans have been known to climb down from the trees, untie the boats, and row them down a river.

Orangutans must learn everything they will need to know to survive for a lifetime during the years they spend with their mothers. (They have the longest childhood of all the great apes — and that's probably the reason why.) For example, various fruit trees throughout the rainforest ripen at different times, and orangutans seem to remember the routes and timetables they followed with their mothers. They don't look for these fruits willy-nilly; they simply seem to know exactly where to go and exactly when to go there.

Parenting skills are another story. Since orangutan females leave their mothers at age eight but don't have their own babies until four to seven years later, many first-time mothers have to rely on instinct. If they stayed around long enough to watch their own mothers take care of another baby, they have a head start. But they can often pick up parenting pointers by watching how other mothers interact with their babies when they see them from time to time in areas where food is plentiful.

Chapter 5
Orangutans in the World

Where Orangutans Live

The **green** areas show where orangutans live.

Scientists have found fossils indicating that relatives of modern orangutans existed about two million years ago. It is believed that they roamed over most of Southeast Asia, including the forests of southern China, Vietnam, Thailand, Cambodia, Laos, the Malay Peninsula, and all the nearby islands. Today's wild orangutans can be found only on the islands of Sumatra and Borneo.

The Sad State of Orangutans

Man has been the orangutan's worst enemy. As people took over more of the rainforest for logging, mining, and farming, this solitary ape lost its habitat and food supply—80 percent of the forests have been destroyed since 1980. In the late 1990s forest fires took their toll, destroying more than one third of the orangutan population in Borneo. Worst of all, poachers killed mother orangutans to capture their babies and sell them to zoos or to keep as pets. Since orangutans are the slowest breeding mammals in the world, their numbers cannot be replenished quickly. Scientists estimate that the population of 300,000 orangutans in 1900 has been reduced to 20,000 today.

The Future of Orangutans

The orangutan in Sumatra is listed among the "25 most endangered primates," according to the World Conservation Union's 2004-2006 report. The Bornean orangutan is also endangered. Scientists worry that the damage done by the tsunamis of 2004 may cause people whose land was flooded to try to take over areas where the great apes live.

To save the orangutan, we must save its habitat. That involves educating people who live in the area, helping them find ways to support themselves economically, and rehabilitating captive orangutans so they can be released into the wild. Some scientists believe that unless we act now to protect them, the orangutan will soon be extinct in the wild. After having lived on earth for two million years, they may be gone in less than ten.

Fast Facts About Orangutans

Scientific name	*Pongo pygmaeus* (Bornean) *Pongo abelii* (Sumatran)
Class	Mammalia
Order	Primates
Size	Males stand 3 to 5 feet tall Females stand 2½ feet tall
Weight	Males 130 to 200 pounds Females 90 to 110 pounds
Life Span	About 35 years in the wild Up to 60 years in captivity
Habitat	Rainforests of Sumatra and Borneo

Orangutans are the only great apes that live in Asia. Chimpanzees and gorillas live in Africa.

You Can Do More

Become a member of an organization that works to protect orangutans and their habitat. One such group is Orangutan Foundation International. There are many others.

Glossary of Wild Words

aggression angry or threatening behavior

canopy the upper layer of trees that forms a leafy ceiling in rainforests

DNA coded material in the cells of our bodies that determines what we look like and how we act and is passed down to our children

dominant the most powerful or strongest

endangered a species of plant or animal in danger of becoming extinct

extinct having died out and ceased to exist

fossil the outline or remains of an animal or plant from an earlier era, often found inside a rock

habitat the natural environment where an animal or plant lives

The Family Name

Orangutans are members of a scientific family called *Pongidae*. Chimpanzees and gorillas are in the same family.

intruder someone who enters an area where he or she is not wanted

mammal an animal with a backbone and hair on its body that drinks milk from it's mother when it is born

poacher a person who hunts animals or fishes illegally

predator an animal that hunts and eats other animals to survive

primate a mammal with a large brain and complex hands and feet

rainforest a hot, humid tropical forest where it rains frequently

species a group of plants or animals that are the same in many ways

territory an area of land that an animal considers to be its own and will fight to defend

tsunamis huge ocean waves caused by an underwater earthquake or volcano that can cause serious flooding on land

Index